SUSAN LA FLESCHE PICOTTE

by Laura K. Murray

PEBBLE
a capstone imprint

Pebble Explore is published by Pebble, an imprint of Capstone.
1710 Roe Crest Drive
North Mankato, Minnesota 56003
www.capstonepub.com

Library of Congress Cataloging-in-Publication Data.
Names: Murray, Laura K., author.
Title: Susan La Flesche Picotte / by Laura K. Murray.
Description: North Mankato, Minnesota : Pebble, [2021] | Series: Biographies | Includes bibliographical references and index. | Audience: Ages 5-8 | Audience: Grades K-1 | Summary: "How much do you know about Susan La Flesche Picotte? Find out the facts you need to know about the first American Indian to become a doctor. You'll learn about the early life, challenges, and major accomplishments of this important American"-- Provided by publisher.
Identifiers: LCCN 2021016010 (print) | LCCN 2021016011 (ebook) | ISBN 9781977132109 (hardcover) | ISBN 9781977133120 (paperback) | ISBN 9781977154965 (pdf) | ISBN 9781977156587 (kindle edition)
Subjects: LCSH: Picotte, Susan LaFlesche, 1865-1915--Juvenile literature. | Omaha women--Biography--Juvenile literature. | Indian women physicians--Nebraska--Biography--Juvenile literature. | Women social reformers--Nebraska--Biography--Juvenile literature.
Classification: LCC R154.P53 M87 2021 (print) | LCC R154.P53 (ebook) | DDC 610.92 [B]--dc23
LC record available at https://lccn.loc.gov/2021016010
LC ebook record available at https://lccn.loc.gov/2021016011

Image Credits
Alamy: History and Art Collection, 26, Science History Images, 8; Associated Press: Omaha World-Herald/Julia Nagy, 24; Courtesy of Hampton University Archives: 19; Getty Images: Archive Photos, 15, Corbis, 9, Universal Images Group/Photo12, 16; Granger: Sarin Images, 10; Library of Congress: 13, 21; Scotts Bluff National Monument: William Henry Jackson Collection, 6; Shutterstock: Alex Landa (geometric background), cover, back cover, 2, 29; Smithsonian Institution: National Anthropological Archives, cover, 1, and 5 (#NAA INV 00691200), 7 (#GN 4501), 11 (#GN 4473), 17 and 29 (#GN 4503); Wikimedia: Ammodramus, 25, Joelwnelson, 22

Editorial Credits
Editor: Erika L. Shores; Designer: Elyse White; Media Researcher: Svetlana Zhurkin; Production Specialist: Spencer Rosio

Table of Contents

Words in **bold** are in the glossary.

Who Was Susan La Flesche Picotte?

Susan La Flesche Picotte was the first American Indian doctor. She was part of the Omaha **nation**.

During Susan's life, many people were treated unfairly in the United States. Women, American Indians, Black people, and others did not have equal **rights**. Some people could not do things like go to school or **vote**. But Susan wanted to learn. She cared for the sick. She spoke out to help her people. She made life better for others.

5

Growing Up

Susan was born June 17, 1865, on the Omaha **Reservation**. It is in eastern Nebraska. Susan had three older sisters and an older brother.

Omaha Indian Reservation in 1871

Susan's father,
Joseph La Flesche

The world had changed a lot for American Indians in the 1800s. White settlers had brought sickness. The U.S. **government** made Indian nations move off their lands. It made Indian children go to schools to learn English.

Susan's father was an Omaha chief. He wanted his children to learn the new ways. But he taught them to never forget the ways of their people.

When Susan was 8 years old, she saw a sick woman die. A white doctor did not help the woman because she was Indian. After that, Susan wanted to become a doctor. She would take care of people.

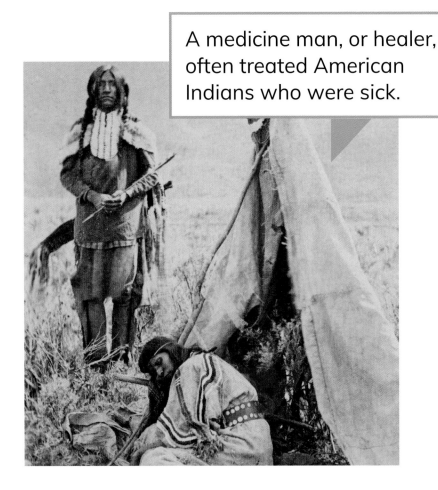

A medicine man, or healer, often treated American Indians who were sick.

Omaha girls at a school in Pennsylvania in 1876

Susan went to the reservation school until age 14. Then she went to a school for girls in New Jersey. At age 17, Susan came back home. She taught at the reservation school. Susan spoke several languages. She liked to paint and play piano too.

Becoming a Doctor

At that time, many people said women could not be doctors. They said women were not smart enough. Susan did not listen. She still wanted to become a doctor. But school cost a lot of money.

Women were taught to be nurses to work with doctors who were mostly men.

Alice Fletcher (seated, center) with other women on the Omaha Reservation

On the reservation, Susan took care of a woman named Alice Fletcher. Alice told Susan to believe in herself. She helped Susan get money for school.

Susan went to the Hampton Institute in Virginia. She graduated in May 1886. Martha Waldron was a doctor at the school. She knew Susan could be a doctor too. Martha told Susan to go to medical school. Women's groups and Indian groups gave Susan money so she could go.

Susan went to the Woman's Medical College of Pennsylvania. She finished school early. She had the best grades in the class. In 1889, Susan graduated at age 24. She was the first American Indian doctor.

Students at Hampton Institute learning about the human body around 1900

Helping Everyone

Susan worked in Philadelphia, Pennsylvania, for a year. Then she went back to the reservation. She was the doctor at the school there. She taught students how to stay healthy.

Soon Susan was caring for the whole community. She was the only doctor for hundreds of miles.

Susan worked many hours each day. She went to sick people's homes. She walked or rode a horse. Later she used a **buggy**. People trusted Susan. She helped with all kinds of problems.

Omaha people in
Nebraska around 1900

In 1894, Susan married Henry Picotte. He was from the Sioux nation. Susan was 29 years old. Soon Susan set up her own doctor's office. She did not turn anyone away because of their skin color. She cared for everyone.

As a doctor, Susan cared for people like this Omaha woman and her child.

Susan and Henry had two sons. They were named Caryl and Pierre. Some people said Susan should quit her job. They thought a woman should stay home with her family. But Susan kept being a doctor. Sometimes she brought her sons along.

Fighting for Care

In 1905, Susan's husband died. Two years later, Susan built a house in the town of Walthill on the reservation. She kept a lamp lit in her window. It showed that people could always come for help. Her home became a meeting place for the community.

Many people were sick on the reservation. Some had sickness in their lungs. Others were sick from **alcohol**. Susan saw people's pain. She taught them how to stay healthy. She spoke out for their rights.

Susan's house in Walthill

Susan became an important leader for her people. She met with government leaders. She spoke out against alcohol. She got help to keep places clean.

In 1909, the government said the Omaha people could not be in charge of their own lands. The Omaha thought that was unfair. They chose Susan to lead a group to Washington, D.C. She stood up for their rights. Susan also helped women and children keep their family lands.

U.S. Capitol in Washington, D.C., around 1910

Dr. Susan La Flesche Picotte Memorial Hospital in Walthill, Nebraska

Susan dreamed of having her own hospital. People gave her **donations** to pay for it. In 1913, she opened her hospital in Walthill. It was the first reservation hospital to not use money from the government. The hospital helped everyone who needed care.

Susan had health problems for much of her life. In 1915, she got sick and did not get better. On September 18, 1915, Susan died in Walthill. She was 50 years old.

Remembering Susan

Susan's hospital stayed open until the 1940s. Today, the building has a museum inside. It has information about Susan and her work. People can learn about the Omaha and Winnebago people there. Susan's house still stands in Walthill.

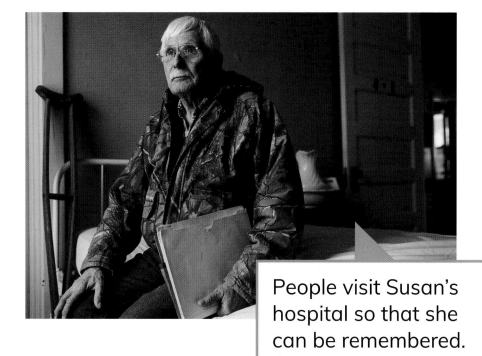

People visit Susan's hospital so that she can be remembered.

Susan's house in Walthill as it looks today

Susan is an important part of American history. But many people do not know about her. There are no buildings or streets named for her.

Today, some people want to tell about Susan's life. They want others to know all she did. They remember how Susan fought to keep others healthy. They speak out for the health of all people.

Susan La Flesche Picotte cared for others. People said an American Indian woman could not be a doctor. But Susan showed they were wrong. Other women helped her. She learned all about health and medicine. She worked to make people's lives better.

Important Dates

June 17, 1865	Susan La Flesche is born on the Omaha Reservation.
1886	Susan graduates from Hampton Institute in Virginia.
1889	Susan earns her medical degree. She goes back to the Omaha Reservation to be the only doctor.
1894	Susan marries Henry Picotte.
1905	Susan's husband dies.
1907	Susan builds a home in Walthill, Nebraska.
1909	The Omaha people choose Susan to lead a group to Washington, D.C., to speak for their rights.
1913	Susan opens her own hospital on the Omaha Reservation.
September 18, 1915	Susan dies in Walthill, Nebraska, at age 50.

Fast Facts

Name:
Susan La Flesche Picotte

Role:
doctor

Life dates:
June 17, 1865 to September 18, 1915

Key accomplishments:
Susan was the first American Indian doctor. During her life, women and American Indians were not treated equally. Susan became a leader in the Omaha community. She fought for the health and rights of the Omaha people. She cared for everyone who needed help.

Glossary

alcohol (AL-kuh-hahl)—a colorless liquid found in drinks such as wine and beer

buggy (BUHG-ee)—a light carriage pulled by one horse

donation (doh-NAY-shuhn)—something you give to help without getting anything in return

government (GUHV-urn-muhnt)—the group of people who make rules and decisions for a country or state

nation (NAY-shuhn)—a group of people who live in the same area and speak the same language

reservation (rez-er-VAY-shuhn)—an area of land where American Indians moved after having to give up their homelands

right (RITE)—something that everyone should be able to do or have and that the government shouldn't be able to take away, such as the right to speak freely

vote (VOHT)—to make a choice

Read More

Ignotofsky, Rachel. *Women in Science: 50 Fearless Pioneers Who Changed the World.* New York: Ten Speed Press, 2016.

James, Emily. *Elizabeth Blackwell.* North Mankato, MN: Capstone, 2017.

Internet Sites

Medicine Woman: PBS
pbslearningmedia.org/collection/medicine-woman/

Nebraska PBS: Medicine Woman
netnebraska.org/basic-page/television/medicine-woman

Susan La Flesche Picotte: Now You Know Nebraska
youtube.com/watch?v=igeXhyTlvP

Index